CELEBRATIONS
Around the World

by Ellen Lawrence

Ruby Tuesday Books

Published in 2026 by Ruby Tuesday Books Ltd.

Editor: Mark J. Sachner
Design & Production: Tammy West

Photo credits:
Alamy: 11 (Tim Gainey), 14 (Louise Batalla Duran), 15 (Xinhua), 21 (Zuma Press Inc); Corbis: 18; Getty Images: 18–19; Public Domain: 16; Shutterstock: Cover (Willy Sebastian), 4L (Drazen Zigic), 4R (Lano Lan), 5 (Kobby Dagan/ChameleonsEye), 6–7 (konstantin belovtov), 8L, 8R (Mcimage), 9 (Radoslaw Lecyk), 10 (Mazur travel), 12 (nana77777), 13 (liu yu shan), 16 (Pierre Jean Durieu), 17 (Pierre Jean Durieu), 20 (JeniFoto).

Library of Congress Control Number: 2024949099
Hardback ISBN 978-1-78856-549-3
Paperback ISBN 978-1-78856-550-9
ePub ISBN 978-1-78856-551-6

Published in Minneapolis, MN
Printed in the United States

www.rubytuesdaybooks.com

The picture on the front cover of this book shows children in Malaysia receiving a gift of money from their mother during their Eid al-Fitr celebrations. To discover more about this festival, turn to page 14.

CONTENTS

Words shown in bold in the text are explained in the glossary.

All the places in this book are shown on the map on page 22.

Everybody Celebrates

All over the world, children and their families take part in celebrations.

During the eight days of Hanukkah, Jews celebrate by lighting candles and giving gifts.

These children in Malaysia are giving a gift to their neighbor at Christmas.

A fun way to celebrate is to take part in festivals and parades.

The Day of the Dead is an important holiday in Mexico. Families take candles, flowers, food, and other gifts to the graves of their loved ones. Children and adults dress up in costumes with skull faces to take part in parades.

In Australia, First Nations people celebrate their history and **culture** during the Laura Quinkan **Indigenous** Dance Festival.

Up Helly Aa

About 1,000 years ago, the Scottish Shetland Islands were home to **Vikings**.

The new year festival of Up Helly Aa celebrates this history with a parade.

People dressed as Vikings walk through the town of Lerwick carrying burning torches.

At the end of the
parade, the Vikings
march around a huge
model of a Viking ship.
Then they throw their
torches onto the
ship and set it
on fire.

New Beginnings

At Chinese New Year, people put the past behind them and celebrate new beginnings.

Chinese people wear new clothes and clean their homes to sweep away bad luck.

Families get together to enjoy large **feasts** and watch fireworks.

Children receive gifts of small red envelopes that contain money.

A Chinese New Year parade in San Francisco

Let's Celebrate Holi!

In India, the arrival of spring is celebrated with the Hindu festival of Holi.

On the night before Holi, people sing and dance.

They roast chicken, coconut, and popcorn on bonfires.

The next day, everyone throws powdered paint and colored water at each other in the streets.

Powdered paint and spices for sale in a market

The **custom** of throwing colored paint comes from a story about the Hindu god Krishna. It is said that when Krishna was a little boy, he threw colored water over milkmaids who were milking cows.

Boys covered with paint

Picnics and Hanami

When pink and white blossoms appear on cherry trees, people in Japan know it's spring!

They gather in parks to enjoy the flowers and have picnics with their families and friends.

People in Japan have celebrated cherry blossom time for hundreds of years.

Cherry blossom picnic food

The Japanese custom of visiting parks and gardens to see and enjoy the cherry blossoms is called hanami. "Hanami" means "flower viewing."
Cherry blossom viewing and picnics
13

Ramadan and Eid al-Fitr

Ramadan is a very important month for Muslims.

During daylight hours, adults and teenagers fast, or don't eat.

People pray and try to give up bad habits.

The end of Ramadan is celebrated with a festival called Eid al-Fitr.

The greeting *Eid Mubarak* means "blessed Eid."

On the first day of Eid al-Fitr, families and friends gather to eat a special daytime meal.

Children in Pakistan enjoying a carousel ride during Eid al-Fitr

The Naadam Games

It's mid summer in Mongolia and time for Naadam!

Naadam festivals, or games, are held throughout Mongolia.

Each festival begins with a big parade.

Then competitors take part in Mongolia's three favorite sports—wrestling, archery, and horse racing.

An archery competition

A wrestling competition

Some of the
Naadam horse races
are 17 miles (27 km)
long. All the jockeys,
or riders, are children.
Some of the riders
are just five
years old!

The Cattle Crossing

The Fulani people of Mali, in Africa, are cattle **herders**.

Many Fulani men live miles from their families for most of the year.

They walk from place to place, finding grass for their animals.

In December, the herders and thousands of cattle return home by crossing the Niger River.

A herder swimming with his cattle

The herders' families gather on the riverbank to welcome them home.

The time of the cattle crossing is a great celebration. Fulani families celebrate with music, dancing, and feasting.

19

A Thanksgiving Feast

Every November, people all over the United States celebrate Thanksgiving with family and friends.

In 1621, the Pilgrims and their Native American neighbors shared a feast to celebrate a good harvest.

Americans think of this as the first Thanksgiving.

Today, people still enjoy a Thanksgiving feast of turkey, cranberry sauce, mashed potatoes, and pumpkin pie.

A Thanksgiving dinner at a center that helps those in need

Not everyone has a place to live or enough money to buy food for a Thanksgiving dinner. Many people help out by cooking Thanksgiving dinners for others who are homeless or living in poverty.

21

Welcome to My World

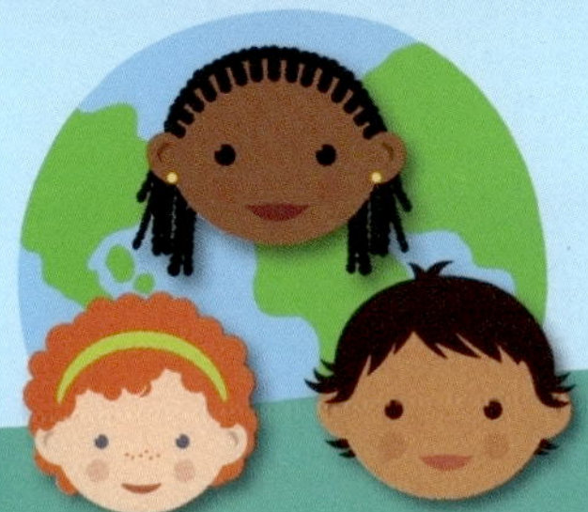

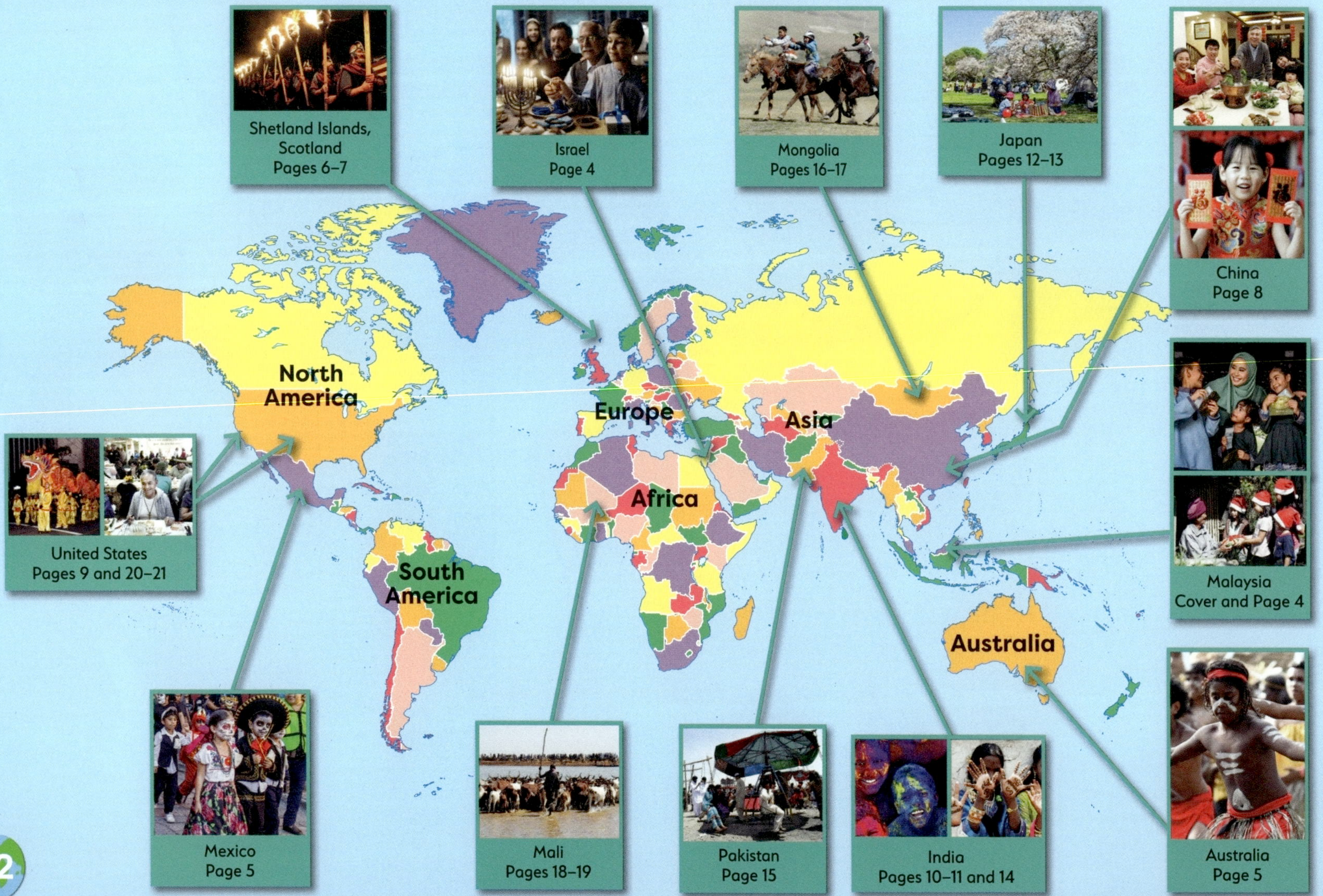
Shetland Islands, Scotland
Pages 6–7
Israel
Page 4
Mongolia
Pages 16–17
Japan
Pages 12–13
China
Page 8
North America
Europe
Asia
Africa
South America
Australia
United States
Pages 9 and 20–21
Malaysia
Cover and Page 4
Mexico
Page 5
Mali
Pages 18–19
Pakistan
Page 15
India
Pages 10–11 and 14
Australia
Page 5

GLOSSARY

culture
The beliefs and way of life of a group of people. For example, celebrations, food, and clothes are all part of a group's culture.

custom
A particular action or way of doing something that has not changed in many years.

feast
A large meal with many different foods that is usually in celebration of a special occasion.

herder
A person who spends their life caring for animals that are raised for food, milk, or skins. Herders move, or herd, their animals from place to place so the animals can find food.

indigenous
Living in a land from the earliest times.

symbol
An item, picture, or sign that stands for something else. For example, an X is the symbol for a kiss. Dragons are symbols of good luck to Chinese people.

Vikings
A group of people who lived about 1,000 years ago. They came from Norway, Sweden, and Denmark. The Vikings were sailors and warriors. They settled in many parts of Europe.

INDEX